The Fragrant Blue Garden of Saints

Stephanie Chang

RED MARE
PRESS

THE FRAGRANT BLUE GARDEN OF SAINTS

Edited by Elyssia Nguyen and Sara Dudo.

Cover design by Emelie Mano.

Interior design by Julianne Johnson.

Red Mare Press / Discover New Art, LLC
70 SW Century Drive, Suite 100442, Bend, Oregon 97702

www.redmarepress.com

Red Mare Press is a division of Discover New Art, LLC.
The Red Mare Press name and logo are trademarks of
Discover New Art, LLC.
The publisher is not responsible for websites (or their content) that are not owned by the publisher.

ISBN 979-8-9939024-1-8

Printed in the United States of America.

CONTENTS

End Times Theory   1

Tall Poppy   3

Our Lady of Perpetual Rot   6

The Fragrant Blue Garden of Saints   8

Lome Lake   10

The Birth of Venus in Beijing   13

Moonflower   14

Rock Face Elegy   15

Euphemism   17

Self-Portrait as Rain   20

For Julián

"Are you that blue light?"
—Mitski

"I used to think that saints were saints
because of a suffering that removed them from their bodies
but then I took too much acetaminophen and realized
it could happen to anyone."
—Kaylee Young-Eun Jeong

"My religion makes no sense
and does not help me
therefore I pursue it."
—Anne Carson

End Times Theory

It is so cruel to call me without warning. In the kitchen,
I take a jar, fill it with water. I dump in the ends of spring

onions, their simple physics. There are a thousand ways
to say *I love you*, even on the phone, even as you say nothing

at all. How are you doing? The headlines say the world
could end any moment now. Myself, I have enjoyed

every selfish and stupid thing—apples, Red Delicious,
and prosecco, too. For a while I wrote you letters.

But I have kept busy. Going outside to water the flowers
in my underwear, quitting my day job, just two minutes

left on the clock. End times theory says you may find
that you lose a bone or two every time you go to bed.

This is normal and no cause for concern. Still, I confess,
I am terrified. For years, I met every morning thinking

I am not yet myself in this life. Now it is August
and I am all of myself I will ever be. The same way

women are born with all the eggs they will carry
in their lifetime, meaning I have always been a part

of my mother; her mother before her. *Do you want
to cry?* Tell me this has nothing to do with explosions

or science. *I don't think so.* Tell me about the dream
you had when we first met, where all the bones

in my body were teeth, my limbs your only light source.
You called the next day, crying. *Is it over? Are we done?*

End times theory says it will feel like a quick pinch.
Do not be afraid, nothing can save us now, et cetera.

It can't be what we know. Come, sing the orchids
and crosswalks to sleep. Say it is the last Monday night

of our lives. Whatever time we have left is lovely
and ridiculous. Touch me and live another day.

This can be a world where my voice does not drown
in static. I close my eyes, imagine you pulling up

to the driveway. We stay up late and sleep in.
I read dirty magazines and get drunk in the bath,

leave the water running. You leave thirty-seven
voicemails to everyone who has wronged us

ever. We will open the windows: what we see will break
our hearts, which I wager are already on their way out.

Watch the world unsuture itself from the shores
of the universe we once trusted to keep us safe,

until the earth is nothing but a vanishing point.

Tall Poppy

Late November. Flowers scar across the field when I blink.
　　　　I am not yet myself in this life. *God loves you but not enough*
to save you, says Ethel Cain. God loves me enough to save

my mother, but not me too. I know this already—
　　　　I have read the books. I spent a whole summer
learning about medieval beasts, imagined myself

among them. All that gilt ferocity. God-smug flesh.
　　　　Bee-eaters, fig-peckers, mothers, too. My mother
once told me I was born enamel. A glowing thing

that burned through her belly like a molten star.
　　　　Or: a pebble in the undercurrent of a deadly river.
The story is never the same. Sometimes I don't

call her back for weeks—I stay in bed instead
　　　　of going to class. I lay there and dream I am
a poppy: catatonic with beauty, encircled by flies.

Fickle as belief. In medieval literature, poppies
　　　　originate from dragon's blood. My hands flay
the pages. I force myself to write about home

without throwing up. Nothing left to the imagination:
　　　　A clean, working kitchen. A Christmas card
for everyone but my father. I close my eyes and fetishize

the gravity of my childhood bed, the sound of apples
          cut into slices of apology. I read love poems
as emails rot in my inbox. Again, I have written around

the subject of home. Someone who is not my mother
          tells me I am a good daughter. Someone else's mother
tells me I am a tall poppy. Meaning: don't lose your head.

Meaning: your hands can be a kind of hometown hero.
          Miles away, I watch a spider spin a thousand ways
home, only to fall seven stories when I open the window—

December, the web embalmed in white.

Our Lady of Perpetual Rot

We drove into town and made a wrong turn. Both times we saw the deer
crumpled and kicked to the curb of the Goodwill parking lot. I was in love

—I think

I can tell you this now. Later that night, I had a dream. You were up
to your knees in crabgrass and cigarette smoke. I was no stranger to want

knowing only what I wanted, despite that strange and walloping feeling
like a wheel of rot orbiting my head. Some sinner I was. Some sin

the color of coffee gone cold but not bad—I liked you so exactly.
In the morning, I texted you to say I am *rotting in bed*. My feet were cold

and faced the window in which the trees wore the sound
of Venetian belltowers, television static, recession pop music.

I tried to remember the dream as if it were a memory : the precious water
in your body glowing : gorgeous ravishing of time. Was it so terrible,

I kept wondering, and yes, it was. Where to begin : the soft stutter
of your eyes, skimming the Midwest sky for a viable source of love.

Your quickness when you bit into the core of an apple, realized it had gone
bad. A violent rush of red. It was *an omen—or just a regular metaphor*, I laughed.

To stare and stare longer : oblivion in full bloom. Sunlight on ordinary
flowers, I know that's what we were. And yet—talking to you, hearing

your voice, but not really, not at all. Touching your shoulder and touching
at once every autumn afternoon in the world. I thought I might have

died in that melancholy, over a shot of whisky with you in my dimly lit
dorm room. So I got on the next train without you. It could have been

a good thing but instead it was maddening. Thank you and forgive me,
I wanted to say. That every time I sat up to get a better look at you,

I could only see the deer. So many times I stopped pretending
to be startled. Turning it over and over in my head: the secret universe

I gazed infinitely down a well. My useless sputtering heart. Still it wants.

The Fragrant Blue Garden of Saints

TESTER

amber, camphor, warm,
spicy, vanilla, patchouli,
aromatic,   balsamic,
earthy,   milky,   grape
leaves, tall grass, fish
bones, flowers, teeth in
the amber, warm, earth,
sweet,   sweet,   sweet,
pearl, rot, ink, wash,
eternal, silk, rot, mist,
mature, storm, verdant,
morning, pyre, fanfare,
sunburnt, scar, petrify,
poison, flower, flower

Stephanie Chang

Lome Lake

In wet roosts, the green sinews of algae sweat themselves on boyish skin.

I am late to the function. Outside of outside, the soft pink on my toes excites

every organism on the rocks. They prune my edges alabaster,

watery red breath, exfoliated afterlives. Take them from me, and go—

picture my voice a translucent scar that runs from my hands to my feet

like a river of spilled milk. Or maybe I am a creature engorged on meadow

jumping mice, hauling my mass and garden-maw to the fire pits,

where I roast the sun on a spit. The Northern Pikeminnow beaten

into crude fossils, reeking the lake from its foundation to pump out ailments one by one. Imagine again, I die cast in chlorophyll. You die thinking this was a poem

before it was a poor expression of love. That day, I softened idly to the world.

I bloomed and was met with a knife to the gut for every fallen tree.

How can I love you before I am born, was the question the elderflowers craved.

Come summer, I watch you lurching toward the grass, baying for foxes

in a season of want. That was stupid, I thought. That was the logic

of dreams; what we were practicing cannot happen in real life.

This is to say, I am the wound and so a world that was.

She is sweetening herself to the wilds, the winds sighed.

Your eyes are the safest place to watch the parasites fester, through the square window

of a cabin fondled by moths, throwing up shadow puppets to cry for help. Stop-motion. Now even the birds startle at the sight of me: forged from flora, teeming with

enamel of predator and prey, a dough moon warmed in the oven of your mouth.

Now, I am spoiled with bites. All excess, I empty to fill up all over again.

The Birth of Venus in Beijing

Heaven pooled around my feet like a skirt / of spilled milk
no wonder, then / the cephalopod singing / in the camera's stark flash
gets mistaken for a swan / sui generis / inflection reflected
rejected / This was not my first time / playing beached whale
hemmed to the ocean's hip / symbiotic / Sunday best: / my blue city
of better time / holding her breath in the spaces between
broken glass and strands / of bleached hair / A swan can be a secret
can seem provocateur / siren cry / skinny cigarette / night bruising
me all night / primadonna / the way I was born: 自然
: A scent I never smelled before / tulle at the thrift / herring
bone / swan song / up to my knees / in the enamel clean current
I posed / I picked my teeth with plastic ribbing / I believed until
it began to hurt / a coast is a kind of contradiction / intervention—
camera fluttering flashing / serves me reptiles, skin shed
on a platter / a finger in a mouth / I can arrange for flowers / petals
plastered areola / grown from bright pink gum wrappers / like a scene
from a famine / the swan serves to / touch / the way a stranger would
body stuffed / with somebody else's meat / Heaven is hurting
and everybody is watching / camera chattering / Camera
come closer / skin and gum / nothing good / can come of this
nothing worth the hunt / ends up down the alabaster length
of your neck / proud / as portraiture.

Moonflower

In the blue grass, the one who is worth it all. Somewhere in Ohio,
I mistake the field for a sky. I wake to eyes grazed red by wind. This
is the closest thing to love: two turtles blinking across parallel lines.
This is the closest thing to a promise: your palms. Still and still not
swallowed by nightfall. Somebody has braided my hair with lakewater.
Sunlight cinches my waist. The coffee grows cold on the veranda,
a thousand tiny organisms blossoming in the bitterness. It is mine
and mine alone. It is only summer, and possible that I am no longer
promised to you.

Rock Face Elegy

Hair cracked   open on the crag,
   I leaned into the salt lick that shivered
     when touched the first time
        like salps on the shore. Colors teeming
     unceremonial. Days after the rain
  and the wind slackened to sweat
       it went without saying—
    I'd have it my way.

Yes, elegy imminent,
     the sea kind, kelp-battered,
       divine. In high school biology,
   we spooned out the insides of a starfish,
    organs old and indiscernible,
        a god-absent shrine.
I never wanted   to be kissed so bad.
    Does nature have intent?

   Eyes creased: engorged
     gummy blue sky. That useless expanse
fertile with too-bright fanfare. Stars, not surgical
  incisions, I reminded myself.
    Grayest denim wash on the waves,
we split an okay caprese sandwich,
      sky flickering   storm
    as seagulls gagged their doggish sounds

yet. If I were the wild, I'd want properly,
                I thought. Autumn on the bluff,
                        it turns me. Good—
                                I've done my time.
                Nightfall. We waded through the eels of beer
                        bottles, breaking   green and true.
In the sand we found two lone crustaceans
                shaped like vultures and dappled the shades
                        of loosrife. They were not without the other.

                        I picture their stomachs full of crystals,
        piss, rock candy creatures. So science!
                        The tide rearing. I am wild in my want—
        I knew then. Come violent dawn,
we'd glow from within.   Bloat with flotsam,
                                body the radial symmetry
        of spiny urchins. Everything made mortar,
                mortal.   *What is your want?*

                        Let the water steal my face
                                and erode it with laughter.
                Let us exit the scene holding nothing
        but our wrinkled hands:
ordinary lovers   strolling seaside.

Euphemism

Dawn pooled at my feet. To my astonishment,
          I wept, and where I wept, my tears dried wolf-

Berry on the mattress, which reeked. It was the morning
         After and the garden of saints was deserted.

Evening's feast, unpicked, abandoned when it happened.
         A platter of fruits, too soft so wrong, retching.

The vultures circled the borders of my body. Afternoon
         Came and went, the moon inside my head

Bitten, downed. O tide of calligraphy of opium, echo,
         opium. I lay horizontal and stared at the ceiling

Lying in a sea of spilled ink. After hours, it was impossible
         To imagine help on the way. Instead I slept I baked

Like a pearl in the water, primed for the harvest. A prayer.
         A prayer. Nucleation: turn me bioluminescent.

In wee hours, I bleached my hair the color of the dead.
         Runaway worms clotted the drain. All the way down,

I pictured a city of crushed lilies. They play dead,
         Wintertime to be believed. A field of white flowers

Holding still for centuries. To enter the city, you must
         darken your breath. You must coax the artifacts

From your flesh: the precious metals, the silver coins,
        The sculpture rubbed raw for posterity. A spoil of war—

Waiting to spoil. Yes, that's what I was. Yes, and what
        comes after? From the land of the living, yes

I wait for you to spoil in the soil you made of me.

Self-Portrait as Rain

i melt

myself a dress

of mirrors / little lakes

courting a corpse / the way thunder breaks

its knee on weathervanes / i can't say / how happy

i am out here / warbled out of wet / heaven's spit exiled

i flush / blue bourbon / all over the carpet / i play stowaway

perched on a poncho / i smile / tarnished teeth / i just want to hold a

permanent shape / if i could hold myself / along perpendicular lines / tongue

forked four ways / once / i starred / in that film about a car / lonely & blurred across a green-screened highway / the window / false / failing me / as i evangelized

about the birth / of oceans everywhere / there's blood / i parasite my body

by smashing it to puddles: / brightest fanfare / confetti of bullet holes

a birthright cut from watercress / how it scarred me / stillborn

o molecule / silver me a storm / to fall / in love with

to fall away from / for good.

ACKNOWLEDGMENTS

Sixth Finch: "End Times Theory"

Tinderbox Poetry Journal: "Our Lady of Perpetual Rot"

HIKA Magazine: "Self-Portrait as Rain"